For Instance

T0308062

For Instance

Eli Goldblatt

Woodcuts, Wendy Osterweil
Drawings, Michael Moore

chax / tucson / 2019

ISBN 978-1-946104-16-8

Chax Press
1517 N Wilmot Rd no. 264
Tucson Arizona 85712-4410
USA

Chax Press books are supported in part by a fund at the University of
Houston-Victoria, and largely by individual donors. Please visit *https://chax.
org/membership-support/* if you would like to contribute to our mission to
make an impact on the literature and culture of our time.

Author Acknowledgments:

Thanks go to these journals
"Parables of Cold" in *88: A Journal of Contemporary American Poetry*
"The Miner" in *Cincinnati Poetry Review*
"Platform." *The Pinch*
"A Slender Singer." *Ixnay Reader*

The stories told or alluded to herein are true, fictionalized, made up, or
dreamt. Many thanks to Charles Alexander for his help as an editor and
friend. The stories told or alluded to herein are true, fictionalized, made up,
or dreamt.

For Wendy, at all times

What is the best thing to do now? *The book is looking forward, with empty hands, toward you. It is grounded in this failure to begin. Death is little, dying large.*

Gil Ott

These are merely instances.

Wallace Stevens

Table of Contents

III. Lilac

I. A Slender Singer

Thirteen Geese

Why resist the poem's whispered end?
Sail out into open water, hoping to find
arches & vaults, tons & inches, ivory &
lead inside the salt waves' high cloudless
sky—Atlantis, the Robber-King's den, a
train between Berlin & Delhi—willing
yourself to doze, dreaming a great world
on top of this bleak one. A palace of empty

courtyards, abandoned sanctuaries, woven
carpets fashioned by hand years ago but not
yet worn, stone floors warm to bare feet.
Thirteen geese, representing a martyr's years,
gabble thru the little garden within cloisters. I hear
singing in rooms ahead but no one appears. Neither

icon, scroll, nor arabesque in this medieval church
without God. I feel prayer but see no pious
sign nor supplicant performing ablutions, pass
alcoves hung in animal story tapestries of
linen, murals with their characters dissolving.

Saint Jerome

Imagine Jerome, translating at his desk, drawn in
broken tile, mirror shards, half-round beer bottles
across a factory wall's speckled face. Peach & navy
tines stab fat violet waves, little death's head set among
zebra-eyed poppies arranged in a potbellied vase. A twill
mackinaw drapes the pipe-framed lion lying at his feet.

The R7 train, its shade algebra sliding across ailanthus that lean
out from loading docks & shack roofs along North Philly tracks,
speeds past mural & cracked windows in a warehouse overgrown
with sewer moss. A mackerel sky gone slack, a well-wrought
will tendered before probate to an empty crowd. Measure

the wound's placement but tend the wound, rage to
speak informing speech itself, wireless muscle ripped from
the rib, skin from fatty tissue until contour folds into stench,
somebody's saint on a vellum impervious to flame or flood.

Museum

Behind a locked glass door stands a statue of him on horseback.
Around his half-sized figure photos of his generals, his advisors, his
friends, but of course one can't read the captions because the glass
door's locked. Down the surrounding hall cases display swords,
pikes, blunderbusses, armor—clean, worked steel—& at the modern
end cannon, carbines, anti-tank & anti-aircraft guns. Along the way
mannequins present arms wearing uniforms from European wars.
Here, even in Barcelona, Franco won. War grows in the mind; my
boy emerges into sunlight stabbing, punching, blasting his enemies
in the courtyard of this domesticated castle to which they charge only
a modest entrance fee.

I imagine a small open boat carrying a casket across its gunwales,
head & feet over the water. The rower stops momentarily to drink
from a plastic jug then switches with his partner crouched in the
stern. The new rower resumes the rhythm until they pull thru
insensate waves onto island rocks. It may storm soon, & they'd like
to get back before the lightning starts. The day is hot & boating does
not cool them, but they must pass the casket to the cemetery man
before turning home. Not many will know of the interment, let alone
weep at the grave, but a body must go into the ground, even this
despised body in a plain box.

Platform

Half the molecules in the universe spin in one
direction while the other half absorb the dialogue
of passengers leaning out to wave goodbye from
their compartments. It must be late 40's, no music
to date the photo, their hair & clothing smudged
by the train's sudden lurch forward. I expect it must

be Rome because that's where they met a few years
after the war, but no one is smoking or drinking wine
or denouncing Occupation. Two travelers splendidly
young, the woman looks ahead to the right with curly
hair flowing back (in black & white the hair appears
vermilion), the man below & behind her, looking up

saying goodbye as the cars pull off. My father's hand
paused almost at his thigh, onlookers' coats form a dark
wall. My uncle seems to have snapped the picture late.

Our Predicament

Our predicament marks the turning year
with a 3-inch paint brush dipped in oil-based cyan.
Clapboard tenements perform dressage, this movie's
high school prom set trembles, talking animals
squeal & pool in the flat-screened weather. Battalions
billeted along the bay can't alter the moon mirror by
sliding to the cold side of the bed, but I linger long
enough to climb a metal ladder at a slant & heave
the dead weight over a chain-link fence as the house
settles around our small thirst. Storm at the center

encodes rapture, a pollywog gene silvered to swim simple.
Black ballpoint splotch above the salutation, a blue airmail
from Mexico City dated August '80 reviews the factions
in war bubbling up from mountain & rainforest, Zona
Rosa severed from the selva or ashy tin can streets.

A plane intersecting a cone results in a two-dimensional
figure that swells to a crescendo unmatched by stock rallies
in all but three recessions. Name them. The involuntary
light on your kitchen table resonates with pigments
her palette holds; she paints all night while you dream steep
farm roads in her hand. He says, "Ought to? Fifty-two
weeks in the year & you *ought to* go now?" while the
beatitude that came into her face hardly matches the high
tide & zeppelins already surmounting a watery horizon.
Twelve 40-pound sacks should hold our troops till we can

press up the hill, take the gunner's nest, & summon
villagers to interleave the dead. Geldings find an easy
target, answer a single riddle, & gobblers read dice
in the dark on our swamp's one synthetic patch.

Contrasting Dyes

Request swing mercy over dry ground or relinquish
territory peeking above the map. Cavalry, drifting
& pounding over the plains enough to frighten small
mammals, makes an attractive ingredient in lowly pie
crust administered lip-to-lip in snow or dust (morning
just a little brighter than even 2 weeks ago). I can well
imagine a burst in the sky above those radio towers
near the bagel store. Disruption? You don't know
the half of it. Between my knees & the darkening
shore tide, the tawdry clinic on a narrow street where
she deposits damp murmurs like a factory looming,
waiting for the arson's tooth. Why have they always

been homesick, deaf to all but the most highly decorated?
Winsome lyrics drift across the dance floor, every phrase
shaped to resemble rustlers & staple thorns. Arising from
an ancient grave, demons tap out messages meant to make
you think a switch never closed tho nearly everybody voted

him out of office. Neither monsters nor flux-bound
reapers josh me, rush an answer into the commercial
market then head back to the firmament, an abashed
sensibility but *somebody* likes me. A third of the meat
population sustains the radiation core, driving forward
with a forgetful grin. Don't suppose you suspect this
season, hands in back pockets or arms folded against
a shielded chest. The rays fly thru anything, reveal

flaws & lesions, attack the dumb rice kernels in the brain.
He can scram because that's what patients do, but as far
as more serious manifestations, that'll have to wait till

science catches up to witchcraft. Persimmons & brodchen
under linden trees signify a shift, a brief loosening of
restrictions. Send her sentences to Personnel & let them
file the prose quickly, feed a monastery crowded with
public outcry against leagues, lobbies, alliances, treaties,
bills of lading. Contrasting dyes against a jet black field.

Looking for that opening,

                        that doorway again
into the garden, I blocked the door myself, refused
to turn the key so long the lock froze, & now I'm
dropping sweetmeats at the threshold. Break into
a hayfield beyond the stone wall along the packed
& oiled dirt road to Cummington.

                               Who scales the body
ratchets an event one foot higher. I think & string beads
from ear to ear, but eventually a jangled countertone
provides a plane to Paris.

                          At the baggage claim
our teacher waits for us to start our lessons as soon
as we check into the hotel and manage our first walk
on rainy streets. Once in the park, she picks up a smooth
pebble—cloudy yellow in her bluish, thin palm—& tosses
it viciously at my head. It's actionable, she says, even
collectible. Neither guarded nor revealing talk would
do because nothing so infuriates a web-based audience
like a slain content provider. I wanted to render the silver
pants, her red Converse tennis shoes, darkly roasted coffee
in a cheap porcelain cup (mentality too endearing to name

in the dozing, broken mumbles I used to favor) but later
literary enterprise seemed indulgent, crashing from its
perch among fatty acids, superior pipe tobacco, a diet
many players endorse. You could destroy your power
pack before the police find oil inside the casing to prove

you detonated the device yourself. No stickers on the wall
or belted pants suit dripping dry on the shower rod. How
do I get across the fear mixed with dog spirits evoked by
today's truck bomb?
                    Quiet interleafing belches
in a crowd dulled with self-loathing, health tacked
on a scented astral screen, mellow one month,
singular the next. Endings pert & upturned, a syllabary
prized for its venom, his glock cocked medicinal to the
brain & toxic to the liver.
                         The hope is for a sentence, one
simple tectonic cooperative venture, excluding natural
selection, sprouting puncture vine in an entirely
new rubric.
                         Three & two the count, two
down, runners on the corners go, finances in order, cookware
stowed for the voyage. At Wrigley, a kid cries in the top row
when his new batting helmet won't stay on his misshapen head.

The Realtor

Cast off your costume in this scene & let naked flanks ride over ministries. She never married the waves, knew neither how to fall down nor bop upright. The disembodied voice belongs to an African politician interviewed by the BBC anchor for American news. Caught up in a struggle few on this side of the planet care to plumb, he speaks nonetheless a pungent english as his airtime expires. Then announcers turn to the Mayor's carnival. Temptation crawls in little glass packets, yearning in a form frozen to be licked. Get on with it, baby, don't you know what you like? Young speakers mount the roof of a 70's Plymouth, gesticulate with their stumps or combat headgear, but I glimpse veterans in the crowd shrug off the glittering sweat on the speakers' skin; old ones see only their own spittle, their own blood. She screams, she shines, as the waves prove again and again the same axiom.

Would you be interested in 4500 square feet just because we share the same birth sign? Mustard plants spread over the yard in a succession that could end in maple or even oak. 40 ounce bottles of malt liquor set in a row on the gray divider guiding traffic under the bridge. These are parts from an old Jeep Wrangler; I was trying to sell you something I regarded as real, but you just didn't like my tone. Couldn't hear, couldn't see, couldn't cook your way out. Yet he still wishes to claim the second floor, no matter what the landlord's asking for security. A crunchy center wrapped in wispy sheets harvested from the sea.

Cantankerous at best, the realtor criticizes their every plan & doubts their seriousness. The two women grow angry & threaten to walk away, whereupon he relents but does not apologize. Killer, really, but far more costly than the mackintosh she wore to protect herself. Sex is never the issue between us, but it does illustrate so vividly what we mean. Air we breathe, land we walk on. When they kiss each other's foreheads on the sitcom, a truck honks mocking tunes from a rival show.

What Happened

Old habit, a curmudgeon bent on conquest.
Failing light harbors fishing vessels you can't
tell from pleasure boats if you aren't the sea-
going type. Down the street a hammer falls

less rhythmically, more of a desperate final
flutter before quitting time than an expression
of architectural grand design. When you eat
most fruit, the peel effects closure before you
start, but at the end what sweet meat remains
you sweep into compost, the anthropologist's

prize midden pit. Easy for lightning to trip a fire
in a storm like yesterday's; thinking only to get
the children away from flood water, they had
evacuated the whole garden apartment complex
just when that explosion hit Building 5. One tenant's
car floated & then came down on her peas & carrots.
By morning all their stories had grown so familiar
everyone almost understood what happened. Today

further south the State Fair closed on a dim note
near dusk, a few people hanging around the stalls
to clear up & pack equipment. Winter seems
so inconsequential in the late evening heat.

Parable of Cold

A baker bakes, a carpenter snaps the chalk line
on an eight-foot drywall sheet. What will you do?
What have you done? All winter seemed a prelude
but until now arctic winds never blew the cold
front in. You cross the furnace room,

tap on the gauge, add water to the system. That's
not the reason you came downstairs, but you
look around at unused tools stored in open bins,
canned goods shelved row on row. You resist
the urge to give it up, to make a lesson appear
on the last line or crumble ancient powders into
one strong drink. All you want in cold is cold, & yet

desire cannot be hermetic enough—no message, no
alchemy, no celibate without blemish—at the
precise moment when flat meets bright, when
water flows over ruby facets of a class ring
the swimmer wears. She strikes ahead
& each stroke brings new cold.

Cold Frames in Petaluma

Plagued fields in crimson silver angled
beyond tall grasses along a rutted road. Plastic
sheeting over cold frames, rusted discs, & a late
70's Ford truck beside rows recently plowed
show off the blood-filled earth where seed
begins to push up a crop naming its rage.
All three minds fashion each other's accidental

desires—dream, memory, perception—& write
the blast now it's come true: a child running down
a basement corridor, all the building's stairwells
open but you're afraid to look back or turn toward
light. No myth prepares us for these storerooms
on either side like so many monastery cells.
It's a free country, they say, but democracy has
a price & war will be among us in a moment.

I could take a cross-town bus to the cemetery
join my friends there mourning & drinking by
the graveside, roasting corn over an open fire.
Celebrants grow heavy in the neck & midsection,
hardly able to walk into the trees & take a piss.

O, yes, the lady with dancing shoes & a lined face.
I can come no closer to her, water between us
bubbling over flat black rocks & scummy fallen logs.

Sparrow enough

Restoration includes all manner
of chirps, squawks, keenings
within which you find the fit.

Let's think strategically about smuggling—
how they get out, how they get in—stories
that give an artist a knot on the right
side of her neck. Seed pods in her print
form mad space ships on the tiny scale
of love events where blood's exchanged.

                    Waterfall in a bottle, car
containing rainforest. Breeze on the legs
in the mess hall where soldiers won't
admit unauthorized personnel, where a man
nonetheless got in & set off bombs strapped
to his chest. After that could they dream
the news? Celebrity turns into a tapeworm
encased on his wall, guppies spattered all
over the grotto crime scene. It's a steep slide
down to the pit; we note thru razor wire
how healthy the captives grow. If you stay
awake, keep up with the reading, ask questions
in class, it's still cheaper for management
to fire your ass & hire labor by the day.

Walk out on flat stones & let
the creek run over your boots.
Paint the whole scene magenta
& green

        (know what I mean?
eat a crust, plant a vine
catch a snake beside the conveyor
belt & stainless steel vats

      mixing, mixing
yellow they paint the courthouse
or company store).

Cops scribble numbers, radio the
helicopters overhead. Whatever
news we hear is wrong. May
went by, June's soon gone.
I've got to steel myself, be
sparrow enough
to sing inside
all that bombing.

Skin

I practice scarification & I don't.
Willing myself to wound my body
to adorn it seems absurd & yet
the welts, hard little mounds, appear
in lines on my skin or on the skin
I think I wear. I can hardly tell what
I mean anymore; the poem comes
to my mind in the form of a knife.

I crave a language beyond all this talk,
words erupting beneath words that evict
or seduce, dominate or sell. The cicada
crawls from his nymph skin singing,
the empty shell signifying an earlier
state when he still waited underground.

So you wonder
for Julia Blumenreich

So you wonder what happens & how
to measure time. A flute bites at melody
in one voice while the bass grounds sheer
or bastard doings to one sweet spot. A town
watch beacon sweeps witlessly under the phone
wires after cops leave an early morning
bust. Two streets form a T at a school parking
lot fenced off from the playground by chain link.
Young boys stride toward homeroom, their
flat-brimmed caps cocked sideways, their scowls
composed. The breakfast joint's not full when I
drive past; I want to stop for eggs & home
fries, coffee on my way to work but never do.

Quick to temper, slow to cool—the Talmud
warns us most about this disposition—while the sky
over Forbidden Drive could momentarily open up
on us. The least mad collie in the litter still runs like
he's herding sheep toward shelter every evening.

Regarding our friend who shot himself in Texas,
filed correspondence & coded accounts argue that
his eyes could not be so calm in this last photograph.
Sitting on a horse & looking directly at us, he gives
nothing away against the small trees, presenting
a rogue flatness in his undeniably Jewish face.

No one else

Dream, love, where younger could do
but wouldn't try. I reach over to you
thru heat & brackish light, we shelter
each other but no words carry
yesterday's windstorm or today's
cool sun. I envy painters only
in this: they follow color along
silt layers & gem gravel, keep
floods back, prop windows open.
Everyday we travel, every day
we settle into curve & rectangle
but choosing brings us further.

Insulating blinds seal our glass porch tight.
I lift the seal & peek outside, think I see a
swill of tiny green fish swimming in rainwater.
They will surely freeze tonight. I should
change the bulb out there, arrange
the firewood.
                    You reach me,

                              dawn,
give no answer to threat; early
sun won't contradict a field sown
in broken teeth, a ghost print on
the skin. O yes, it's a history

quiz out there, each weather report

hunger on the bridal registry.
No one else guides purchases,
prompts autopsies, turns
the light off when we sleep.

The Miner

Window blew open in the night. Hallway
& upper rooms lost all heat. By afternoon
the blank filled up again: roast chicken, radio
news, potato & carrot soup. Branch fell
in the fog still pond, moon stabbed in a
widowed sycamore. They suggest a melody
we haven't heard, in a key we don't know
to a rhythm we can't mimic or evade. Every
door wants nothing from you, stairs resist
your step. Dim bulbs light waxy walls,
paint attaches spindles to the rail.
Lay your cheek against the mirror;
a miner wouldn't enter such a shaft.

Imaging

The receptionist wonders aloud but can't fix
a time when they'll guide us back to the trailer
for Leo's MRI. Earrings & body ornaments
throw off the imaging, toe wiggles destroy
the picture; this machine marshals energy bursts
to track tears or pulls beneath the skin. We wear
ear plugs while the operator hides behind a steel
door. Shivering past the night nurse who smokes
her last cig of the shift, we head back to the car
more chastened than healed. We carry films
the tech printed out for the doctor to read.

Real war pounds elsewhere, but echoes
hook the light poles, enter newly painted
pews in the corner church thru fresh
stained glass. F-10's & Hondas stay put
in the CVS parking lot, their bitter weight
pressing asphalt into the dirt below. Fear
forms yard & fence, air blazes & friends

go quiet. Beasts,
dancing fools, green
cicada clinging, marking
time in tune. A message

in deep morning sleep:
Tell us but tell us quickly.

I changed

I changed in a gas station
      put on proper clothes

Club entrance required a military pass
      Wedding guests—black
            jackets, yellow sheath dresses—

seemed joyous enough, uncles
      witty at their brother's expense
            groom sensible to his mother's relief

bride's family smiling on an aisle
      their language not the language
            of the place

Empty Garden

Emptiness isn't abyss enough wherever
you look. In fact, the brushfire that started
in my side yard spread, first to our garage
& then across the bushes to the neighbors'
back door. All around the flames
the children stood—neither dancing
nor singing—but swaying to the
blaze. Vans & trucks gathered
but nobody retreated or even moved
as fire blistered the doors & passed thru.

Small red conical flowers grow from low
plantings around the fountain in our garden.
An electric pump runs all day & night
in the hopes that we'll attract hummingbirds.
We keep sugared water in the feeder,
watch from behind white curtains in the hall.
The tiny birds never appear, won't take
our offerings or nectar from our flowers.

Any Cottage

The world is filled with hidden running water
That pounds in the ears like ether
                                    Kenneth Rexroth

You would wish nothing, say nothing, express
nothing, hope nothing, become nothing, regard nothing,
leak nothing, quash nothing, regret nothing. Let these words
remain on your lips & follow you around as if they belong
to another universe but occupy attention meant for soup
meat or intake manifolds. A crushing bonfire forms at the
margins of a widow's tight smile, a sweetish smell fills the air
around the altar at her waist. Half in shadow & fully armed,
a crowded man emerges from his rowhouse more quantified
than clever, sure his memory records intact the bounding
hell prophets spoke of, the catalytic heaven they tried to
praise. Everything happens so quietly. I barely lift my head

when the pounding stops & vistas once enclosed in foil
swamp the canoes & drive ancient rule-governed behavior
beyond the call of parents & pupils alike. Will you, too, work
against me when you hear the low whistle, when you walk
into a room arrayed with sunfish & carrier pigeons no one
has seen alive since willows took root? It's a terrible

surprise, the sardonic frequency keeping an old broadcast
tower aloft. Any element requires a style, any cottage
houses the perfect sensation. Rexroth walked out over
a ridge, the sun setting onto still dark blue mountains

in front of him. The next morning his words slid down
the paths or leaked away as dawn came on, "the hermit
thrush absent at breakfast"; common city birds began
to sing an estranged song compared to his Whitman-like
rants in Latin & Chinese, Provençal & Greek. By what
lights do we rejoice or mourn? When my mother began to

lose an idiom for even the simplest emotion—fear, say, in
the coffee house that afternoon when nothing more could
be done—poetry would not parse that scattering remorse
in a grammar of deciduous woods or pines above the tree
line, birds we couldn't count, name, or invent in the sudden
afternoon warmth of Rittenhouse Square the April she died.

End of Mysticism

That quest appears too muddy now for fashion
to accompany untouchables into the mine. Terms
suit no one's idea of honor or perfidy. Growling
ill-tempered, the jaguar paced her cage until she
noticed the calf leg her keeper had tossed from
the back passage as we watched.   Many waited
listlessly, but minutes into the contest a bomb
went off under the stage. Musicians left instruments
to burn & leapt into the audience where only a few
turned long enough to catch drummers, trumpeters,
& a flautist while chandeliers crashed onto the plush

red seats. I called their house after the holidays & got
his wife on the phone. She told me they'd pulverized
his kidney stones, & he should be back at work within
the week. He'll want to kill us once he finds out
we altered the requirements while he was sick.
Not that our decision adds up to revolution, but
no agency could leave so many off the rolls & still
maintain the fiction that they advocate for the poor.

Willing or not, each party holds its silence.
Modesty requires no action despite the violence
in every private precinct, in every cubicle on each
floor of every office building in an eight-block radius.

A letter appears on the tent wall
  late that night, shaped like
    a chair, maybe a river

a map of falling cities, turds in the
  water supply, dim gallery
    on my rented retina

A Slender Singer

for Gil Ott

I set out bowls of soup at the wooden table in the narrow dining
room. I can hear the others in the kitchen, still talking and drinking
wine. This evening will go all right. But what about those who
aren't here? The ones we invited but couldn't come, the ones we
didn't think to invite?   I offer puppetry, song, a little history. Steady
rain soaked us all just running from the makeshift theater in the barn
back to the house. I never know how negotiations will proceed after
a performance.

Lump in chest, arms
& gangling legs
unfilled by weight
to walk the planet or
wade into lake frost.
Suddenly again weak,
awaiting diagnosis, named
merely by symptom.
In that bed he calls
for his socks & shoes
ready to go home
heedless of wires & tubes
binding him to this
spot far from poems.

I woke suddenly at 3:05 AM, thinking I heard her voice say "O—are
you already asleep?" I tried to follow her, but she kept disappearing

among apartment buildings. I entered rooms looking for her, asking
if anyone had seen her. She had always just left the party, and I began
to worry she didn't want me around. People intervened and urged
me to join the game show or address the protesting crowd, but I
always needed to get back to the hospital before evening.

The prospect could transpose you
a band playing a march against war

Beat adds counter currents to blood
amber flash or false positives in chorus

Holly, birch, maple in the snow at home
but here we link arms shouting

Sign carriers rush cops, barricades
can't separate bereaved from betrayed

Officer rides a silver horse off stage
where blue barriers keep sound out

A slender singer, a rebel, a dark riverbank. Questions temper glass,
an unkempt beat burns crown into syllabary, constructs in time
a moist canticle. That's for reaching & that's for cantering back.
Police arch over the mendicant's shoulder, repossess his wine. You
get right up to that West Philly door into the party but can't go in;
the stench rises from under the porch. Stamp & scream all you like
but no doorkeep ambles up. Celebrant concludes on key, & out the
barn door swallows slip & dive to catch an evening meal. Coinage

& wreckage spread across the yard, twisted emblem affixed to a
mechanic's cap. Nobody wants the singer's ritual to cease.

He lies on the narrow bed
starved puppet expecting
the throng to sweep him
into neighborhoods where
they serve Mediterranean
salad & clear liquor decanted
from a tall red bottle set
beside pita baked expressly
for his meal. She smiles at
his sudden eyes grown near
& every doctor disappears.

The little self dissolves, the spume can't hold together a minute
as rain falls hollow & cove melts into coastline rock shelf, ocean
covering old clefts. We can hardly stand upright in the storm,
clinging to the dock rail like so many puppets under tall trees. Bulb
light seeps from a trailer parked up the hill. Keeping watch in our
yellow hats & slickers, desire for warm drink & a few kind words
exchanged in the dark.

All bricks in a batch weigh the same;
flat stones differ but can fit to match.
A barn sits atop newly dry-stacked
walls, solid again after a hundred fifty
years. Inside, the children who came
for the show settle into their own idea

of rows & most sit still; fidgety ones
raise their hands to be excused before
the lights dim.

           Morning rain bends red
poppies but does not tatter the petals.
Song, nothing wrong with song.

No matter how much you fracture
harmony & fear takes you, a single
spot burns your forehead—sharp
shooters' beam, mystic ray—but
after curtain rise all adages splinter
away. The slow gesture & quavering
tunes stray above the puppets' waving
hands, barn joists define a church nave.
On stage a bare head & peeled eye arise
from a dumpster beside a brownstone.
A singer in back of the song, singing.

      He hesitated & then entered the workshop. The tools seemed
smaller now after his illness, & he wasn't sure how each of them
shaped wood or metal or cloth. He could feel the dull ache he always
felt when he came into his work space: the desire to make something
new, the fear that he might not be able to manage it this time. Then
forgetting, beginning to follow an unfolding presence. The puppets
hung all around him, sat on shelves, peered at him in pieces from
boxes on the floor. The bins still held scraps of cloth stored by color
or pattern, and his sewing machine waited beneath a window along

the long wall. His table was neatly cleared—magnificent expanse—
and chisels and knives stood in racks beneath the window. He had
left the room as he always left it, clean for the next day's work if not
fully ordered to the mind of a visitor new to a puppet shop.

He picked up a mallet, or tried to. His hands no longer closed
around the handle, and he had to pick it up with his fingertips. He
could not grasp it securely enough to hold the weight, and it dropped
back onto the face of the table with a *thuck* that sounded like the
closing of a car door. He hadn't turned on the light when he first
came in, and he realized the afternoon sun wouldn't last much
longer. After all, it was already nearly winter though he hadn't been
in the shop since late spring. He looked out across the yard, to the
barn where he used to give performances. Bats and swallows began
to swoop in the twilight air. He could no longer see the pattern on
the armor of the Norse goddess or the mudcloth jacket of the African
diplomat.

We act in a movie—sentiment & counter
sentiment—tamped, packed, or sliced
in an ice storm on a city street. Officers
survey the murmuring masses, the placards
& effigies, from high on their blue-draped

horses. You blink in hospital light, the gown
slips off your thin pale shoulder, reveals color
coded wires leading to monitors above your
head. At the nurses' station they keep an eye
on it all, watch the rise & fall, count the body's

tides; Congress can't pass a law to right
this ship. Around the neighborhood, he
says, I'm alien but they still treat me well.
They know a refugee needs shelter, even if
he's running from his own blood. Doctors

string you along, nurses expect you to listen,
aides have me breathing into blue tubes. I'd rather
be a puppet in a show of my own devising.

Calendar

Woodcuts by Wendy Osterweil

January

Those brow furrows,
infant fingerprints
in a catacomb mind
Sticks & empty thistle
barbed against an
angry snow,

blessed curse to
parallel cunning
   Winter
seeks to obliterate
hooked pods, the
only verdure
left over

March

Bound in a tendril plane
& gripped at every
spade's edge, ground &
sky can't shake loose
one from another
       Seeds break
rock while Gaudi's

guard-head oversees
art cast out of
native dirt
          Green
troops float south
against commanders'
first plan—the Turks
wouldn't have us—but

in this plot stems lift
ice & the buried
burn upward

May

Leaves beaded,
trumpets pendent
above simple petals
underfoot
            All you've got
this night, put under lock
because war unfolds
altho far from here

It's a good world
this evening after
another rain
            You
could turn around
& go back to no
names, almost
feel the present
clouded in dark

tones diminished
to a sleeping key

July

Open-mouthed
etched on stone green
leaves by acid
sun, offspring
make a meal

of worms & grubs their parents fly in twelve times a day. The artist
can't stop watching for hours day after day, discovering that parents
carry off the young birds' feces in white sacks, seeing the offspring
double in size. She draws them, photographs them, laughs at them,
talks about them, reads about them, dreams about them. Then one
falls out of the nest, the next jumps to a lower limb, a third simply
disappears—all in a morning. No bird returns to the nest on that day
or thereafter.

A line in the place of a bird,
thatched lines in place of a
nest; a token for soldiers
taken in ambush—knowledge
in place of presence—a garment
where a child stood witnessing
battle
       Bees collect pollen not out
of mercy or duty but hard-wired
habit   Drunken summer leans
too far over our porch rail

September

After the petals
pods form, their
forms go solid & stalks
harden against growing
cold   Little fruit in a
garden for the eye but
much to structure space
in dark afternoons you
picture again & again

One cannot expect to be
in a place forever as I
would stand here, write
here   You layer me leaf
over leaf, each stem bent
in its history with winds

Little that's noble now
in occupation, & spot
bombs kill soldiers, newly
uniformed police, a father
hurrying to buy fruit
from young men in
early market weather

Two Dreams

What happened inside this shed?
Blue stars spray painted large & small across
corrugated sheet metal walls, the plywood
floor gives way at each step, rolls of insulation
stored in the joists just below the roof where
a child barely old enough to conjure a stone
sits waiting for his mother to come home.

I am the youngest of three sons in post-war London.
Rats run the streets & threaten to storm into the house
whenever you open the door. Each day the oldest brother,
Paul, who has two teen daughters of his own, leads the middle
son out to the front of the house and locks him into a cage
shaped to hold his body & even his head completely still.
This young man is a piano prodigy—I hear him playing
late at night—& Paul says it's for his own good & the good
of the family; he will attack us if we don't keep him locked up.
I'm somehow supposed to write a novel that will free my brother.
I don't know how to do this or whom to make the main character.

II. Emeralds

All you've heard

All you've heard, captive over 50
years among abandoned forts, granite
crumpled by rain, split by ivy & ice.
Madness counted the decades, dry beans
in a bottle. One reporter served her time
stepping over dead bodies after each blast.

Tempting to mean
nothing, poet, in a garden
viewed between iron bars.

In dream I hadn't come into the room
yet—sun on orange settee, coffee mug
in hand, tune crusting
my ear—caused me to grunt
& wake my dear, for what?

Storm I could only hear at street level
but from the ridge of a cold dune I saw
tensile waves repeating, barely
contained in a painted saucer.

Salt in the Wound

Armored cars beyond the closed airport roll over
cracked dry pavement, the radio reporter says, &
outside my kitchen a hidden bird hazards two quick
notes in dance beat & a twirl. Hummingbird drinks at the
feeder & next door the mom sets off with her kids to school
too late, too late. Time falls like this rain, & I remember
no opinion holds sway among wet lobed leaves of angel's
trumpet. Comfort to think there's no plan; a mother can't

intercede for her son painted above a church nave, within
a fiery lake or God's bright triangle. In truth, neither frog
nor hawk stands a chance against a thresher, & no riot could
stop machines from gathering the harvest. Sometimes
everyone's a real estate broker. Don't talk such nonsense,
little creeper with your cruel verbs, cramped handwriting,
preference for lists: beets & cherries, grilled pineapple,
smoked mozzarella, tomato slices topped with fresh basil
& kosher salt. Soldiers love their MRAP transport,
high carriage & hardened steel underbelly
protecting riders from IEDs buried in the road.

Between Us

Ancient marble crocodiles set along a twisted
stony road. Helicopter overhead traces lightly
inked lines above crested waves swallowing
a narrow boat in the bay, hand at the rudder
obscured by spray. Stairways unhinge, arches
crack. A girl takes off her gas mask, shakes out
her black hair & whispers into her phone,
hoping the boy can guide her home. Workmen
strip off plaster & lathe, step over flocked
wallpaper strewn on apartment floors. Rubbish
heaped in tiny trucks at the curb. They cart away
whole dung hills of cracked amphora, syringes,
cauldrons accumulated in the space between us.

Six fish

for Linda A-K

Six fish play out the wind in her fabric. She
sews the layers together or separates them
into unnumbered latitudes. Hands wander over
rough sand, indelible marks on skin, a maze
for contemplating incidental shadow, rose
scent & ambulance scream. High speed trains
slip thru dark mountains, but my friend & I

drove, stopping to inspect trinkets in a town
off New Mexico 85. Wherever we turned, doors
served a double purpose, selling & buying back.
This is regular, natural. When do you live
in a place for how long? Restless at sunset
in an opera built for sunset, I couldn't control

my habit of seeing disaster. Mountains
don't move, don't even flicker in thin
air among violet scrub, juniper, & pine.

Such narrow passages

Such narrow passages require
        capillary action to enter the
                chamber no bigger than

a cockroach swarm,
        memories pressed against
                cardboard dividers, their

capacity for infinite
        regression at bastard speed
                can't dodge the whiptail lizards

feeding in a darkened lab. Kettle
        provides quiet basso,
                piccolo etching the brain pan.

Far away horse tethered to a ring
        in the red wall, paving stones
                beneath his hooves, spittle—

white sky edged in roofing tile
        dread made flesh among vendors
                or she who is carved love.

I hope the bees survive
        these next winters; we'll need
                the fugues & pollen they carry.

Quantities

1

I sat in a metal cage, a tiny room
defined by a steel frame & heavy
gauge wire painted yellow. Duped.
I felt duped, no matter who came to
visit or what drama unfolded among
my captors. They had put something
over on me or I had fooled myself, but
the result left me in a basement, at the
bottom of an elevator shaft. Neither
hungry nor upset, I stared into the
dim concrete room where my captors
discussed their 5 year plan for me.

2

We had just moved to a new town
& I had not yet memorized our
address. I met a man in the grocery
store who tried to sell me an alternate
cable connection—one that would
bring stories to our tv unlike any
that other people saw—but I put
him off, saying we weren't settled
enough yet to decide. Later I ran
into him again inside an elaborate
house, really a dormitory or

classroom building of a small
college that had once been
a rich man's home. I found
I could float down stairs, but
when we went to eat, no one
knew the dining room we sought.

3

At dinner the other night we talked about
our responses to the art exhibit. A little
tense because someone we all knew had
fallen ill, we found enough opinions and
curious tales to keep up conversation
thru appetizers, the main course, and tea.
When the bill came, the eldest in our party
paid, & I went out into the neighborhood to
bring the car around. The paintings had been
old favorites, but some I once admired
seemed merely ghoulish now. Spring
would be here soon, and couples pushed
baby carriages in the dark despite lingering
piles of dirty snow from last week's storm.

4

In the half-track depot, a corporal fields requests
from the men that his CO denies each following
day. Soft bleached cancers flower fresh on the

coverlet's green & purple. Accidents retell our
futures. Lit from below, the library's colonnade
begins to flicker & tear along the scrim's bias
until we glimpse the feet of the chorus as they
wait to sing. An open door, festooned with dry
garlic & framed by arched arabesques, flattens
to a Persian miniature in the afternoon light.
A mad man digs; another bows his head beneath
a tree jeweled in autumn. A distant violet sky
echoes his prayer, neither angry nor annealing.

5

Travelling separately, they didn't spot
anybody or identify a brand they knew,
but the alarm turned out to be incompatible
with police frequencies, which gave them
a few days head start on their accusers.
Yesterday receded into choppy water until
the last cold waves lapped on the rocky
shore & all went still. Of course the racket
began again, the destroyer god at the right
while on the left sat toothless Memory,
grinning & whispering. By a torch carried
along the pathways, we saw a white bird
inscribing an awkward spiral above our
heads. Just at the point when I remember
the name of their village, my friends laugh
drunkenly & warn that nothing can be

owned, nothing written down. Kids collect
old garments & repurpose them for an
economy based not on money but on sand.

6
I leap down the gravel path that leads
from our Italian hotel to town. An attractive
young woman ahead of me is complaining
her man cannot learn statistics. I realize
I neglected to put on my shoes. Stones begin
to hurt my feet. My wife & son are hungry
& will not want to wait while I labor up
the hill again, but just before I must turn
back, I see my shoes in the path as if
waiting for me. Nearly at the bottom
I recognize I also forgot my shirt; surely
they will frown on an American sitting
bare-chested in a restaurant, drinking wine.
Perhaps I can buy a sleeveless t-shirt
in a tiny store off the central plaza? But
I have left my wallet in the hotel as well.

7
Once a poem comprehends machine
the rest seems easy, unhorrified.
Saying goodbye retains a logic
reserved for the rich, despised
luxury all the more savory for
its wasteful hunger. You look

in another eye. Give chase.
Respect the hollow distance.
Equate marigolds with burning
row homes, broken teeth in a
sleeping head. Watch pictures
on cell phones as if they
will keep time tamed.

Music & Time

Tin screech lingers on the dream screen
from a training film for firing mortars.
Nothing elevates my mood like tunes.
Someone surely must have been drunk
because four passengers died in the crash.
Brace yourself against collapse among ironies:
Glass skyscrapers in a plain winter box. We dug

trenches around shelter-half tents that sleep two.
Wintering here, our patrol leader resisted the
scout troop master. We baked bread in an oven
constructed of sod. Later that night our cathedral
fell in, but we didn't mind by then. Orders came
down to prepare for a hike or strike camp. Why

couldn't we build a lookout tower? They forbade
us even tho we'd foraged materials, including loose
fiberglass, in the abandoned munitions
site all afternoon the day before.

Weeds

How do I brush past vegetal tangle
& find a path under spruce & oak?
Fine conceit for the city—shut pizza shop
or burnt corner bar where deals went
bad—dame's rocket amaranth
fleabane butter & egg yellow wood
sorrel curly dock narrow leaf
plantain purple dead nettle.

      I suspect myself walking
from train to office, unearth flat
sentences hidden in trash. Maybe
I'm a criminal wastrel, locked cell
lurker witnessing burglary & mayhem
mouth taped, arms wrapped in black
plastic I carried into the woods.

Magenta oval aurora & shifting
lime stabs into a night sky I saw
once on screen. Looking up, I stumble
over a stripped Audi, tree of heaven
growing where the engine used to be.

Emeralds

Throw 6 sticks or toss coins, prophet,
listen to the pulse & drink sweet hot
mint tea. No god to stand behind me
whispering evidence on garlic &
vodka breath. A revelation! Gray
weft crosses violet warp, a shawl
hiding what's exposed. I'm on this
red cliff looking over the broken
plain: child & father wash rock bundles
in their wheelbarrow, cloudy emerald
nubs amid limestone waste. Shrapnel
& bloodied school notes in my mind.

Clear green stones heaped on white
paper between miner & jobber, earth
& glass case. Celebrants all
look down at worn hands.

Conjure his fat eyes

Conjure his fat eyes with a pen stroke
cloak dashed in air beside a stream
blood over stones & twigs shaded by
spindly white pine. I've seen hemlocks
more sprightly, but his paunch signifies
many suppers with ancestors, lightest
touch on his brow makes his gut sting.
OK, that's final, you might be thinking

but carry his burlap sack over to the fire
steaming at the corner of the encampment
feel its weight of turnips and roots, a small
rabbit he caught in a trap, & no matter
where you stand the cavalcade comes at
you as if in a dream: bestial droplets
dancing from here to the waterfall;
faded green, sapphire scratches
on the face, onyx & gold studding
purple velour tunic; immense
hands offering rich dirt for rain.

That would be the last we hear of you.
No more aging, no more wandering.

February ice

bursting exactly along downed
twigs & limbs. Wind cannon in
high alarm. Small houses
scream: child asthma, father's
heart attack, workman's bleeding
hand held over a tub. Wicker
basket full of old oak slows my
steps into the house, fireplace
where embers await new wood.

Dark Garden

Everywhere the entrances, garden
doors without keys at a darkening hour,
birds faintly stammering sentences
from a different decade. Don't care to
understand or pitch a tent, testify or
desire among boulders. Once you leap,
one foot comes down you hadn't meant
in a palace reserved for lanterns & kelp.
Squarish face ten thousand strikers wear.
Corn peas beets rotting along the river
where brilliant children pick their meal.

Simple to explain years on the line
blowing a crumpled trumpet. You
fight like an order of egg & sausage:
inside, you find dark matter.

Powder-coated for sleek finish
red or teal blue, steel brocade.
Wind blind everywhere but here.
Why do we honor ubiquity in a god?
Loosen one brooch or another
the gates remain locked, locks
themselves hidden from view.

Detective Novel

Chapter 1

I step into water enough to soak my sandals, then bend down to wash my face. The cave around me isn't entirely dark—the mouth ahead shows morning shimmer on the lake & cracks in the stone ceiling allow early sun to filter thru dank air. Once awake, I remember the night before. Fire rose above the trees & I fled down steps cut into rock, hoping you would follow me while everyone else ran out the gate of the formal gardens. A sweet, oily smell reaches down even to the edge of this underground stream I slept beside. I can't believe my luck now. You wanted to talk to me about something, but I never heard what was on your mind.

Chapter 2

How about we make it square? You share all your sources with me & other reporters, & we tip you off when we're breaking the story. The debates ended before they began; we knew neither candidate could damage anyone but the voters. It seems sad or comic, depending on how close you sit to the door. Several small children crawled around on the linoleum, cats whined for more food, someone slammed a cabinet in the pantry. Keep your spirits in motion & hope we can address the youth this time. The Party will take your questions once the polls close, but don't expect a change in emphasis, let alone a plan of attack.

Chapter 3

A stranger left the duet manuscript on the kitchen table last night. This morning we followed the chord progression, but the lyrics seemed strained, foreign to the tune. With those words, I expected to hear a march or a bass drone like firepower entering air space. I had to chuckle, even tho the violence seemed so present, because I remember when police stopped citizens for no reason & we simply read about attacks in the paper next day.

Therefore a grassy

ridge behind stock
houses on a steep
street above Villa
Spada. Lovers arrive
late for sun's last
rage & owners
allow schnauzers
& labs to run from
scrofulous forest to
curly fence bordering

wild vineyards
waiting for a darker
chance. Too cool
now to sit for
long in clouded
evening, when
dogs follow
their masters
home, we stalk
down past brick
fronts & small
altars to graffiti
porticos deserted
in this district
after dusk.

904

for Joyce Fried

I walk down the hallway toward 904, beige flowerheads pebbling
umber wallpaper, wine carpet running like a stream under my
steps. In the air, stew & roast chicken mix with emollients &
salves. My mother no longer resides among the old, their families
gathering in community rooms downstairs for holiday dinners, their
memories sharp from an éclair seventy years ago but hazy about a
granddaughter's recital Tuesday. We're prancing along Forbidden
Drive beside the Wissahickon, gravel below my horse's hooves, my
fingers woven tightly into the coarse hairs of her mane. Narrow
world, sibilant dismissals, billets emptier than growl. You retain
the authority to arrest me for crimes I may commit, but I will run, I
swear, out of the quadrant. For all the geese, I wear a hat & yet a call
came yesterday I needed to answer—my gums receding so much they
couldn't keep my teeth in place. North of cornstalks in November,
Wisconsin breeze herds the fog among red oaks & sugar maple, the
path tamped down by runners & trudging farmers. So they listen,
so they translate dreams imperfectly, letters etched in reverse or
calligraphy on canvas! We don't think she means what she says at
table any more, but in the next room everyone will understand her
accent. Here 904, but elsewhere—

Tinnitus

You heard a constant
high whine so silence
couldn't dwell in the ear
Then you entered

I say you but mean me
I say me but mean we

Questions wheel around
my little muddled head
toy trams, armored insects
rolled in a metal ball on
hot sidewalk Children
catch each other in their
playground games
        Speech fails

in your absence
your entrance
I mean you
inaccessible by word
or me sitting still
suddenly ancient
in the sun room

Bird cornered

Bird cornered
by a cat pecks
wails, beats
her dusky wings
on pavement.
All transactions
stopped along
this avenue years
ago. Handsome
lady on a poster
mostly torn from
a wall itself
long severed
from its room.

Rubble cannot
order the day. All
anyone can do is
gather when so
much lies
discarded. A
fool's occu-
pation, cat's
cry when bird
slips away.

5 Poems & Drawings

Drawings by Michael Moore

On a Square in Mississippi

I park the car & we walk two blocks
toward the courthouse. Bronze
cannonballs atop fluted columns
guard brick & white trim civil order.
Top cupola reaches across epochs,
judges define property inside while
around the square Lexus & Land
Rovers whip past shops that
clothe the ache.

       South extends a
thousand miles in every direction,
up my skull & down my knees.
I drape skin over naked arms
but cannot pass the test. Daily speech
mixing script & cursive—cur, mongrel
domestic & show—barks phatic slang:
know your place. We order coffee, eggs,
toast but neither bacon nor grits.

Really, could this happen anywhere?
A young white man fires an automatic
weapon in a church, theater, school
or courthouse. A little towering
figure bursts into bloody fronds
among charities, law offices, the only
secular bookstore in town. Suddenly

your dear one is gone, next
conversation or kiss scratched
from the drawing just when
realism matters most.

How would we walk back to our car
thru war history imprinted on
mugs & commemorative towels?
Decades before the amp
dropped inside my cochlea, tiny
hairs swayed to a child's moan
beside a pool, stinger still
clinging to her cheek.

Storm in May's Landing, NJ

Ribosome tales on the collective grid,
nor'easter texts a billowing message
no one reads amid chowder at the
diner & fields turned to bog. Character
flaws in the round Governor bind him
in meters of oily twine two hours south
of New York City. Bomb the opposition
he declaims on breakfast news
for ears tuned to middle C.
Stop teen fights at the mall!

The slide holds cheek cells lit from
below, skewered gene notes set
upon a raft. Lab tech adjusting
her eyepiece at the end of a shift
laments her so late luck. Outside
the vet, rare sedge wrens nest
by a diminutive lake & boats moored
for the night rock sleepers who know
peace barely eight days a year.
Mandolin & steel guitar from a
dockside bar can't warm June rain
traffic blurs & lights bleed off
overlooking cottages onto reunion
celebrants toasting 35 gone years.

88

Anybody's guess how fire started weeks
before renovation began on Wheaton
Plastics—long cement floors braced
by iron columns, church face squared
to the sun in three glass spans—shut
down last century. Old forklift operators
& product inspectors laid off without
severance but the young turned to sorting
fruit or cleaning egg ramekins at casinos
half hour east on the AC Expressway.

Lace forms a migratory pattern, swallows
leaving nest boxes follow dotted lines
to the next paradise. Cast your 10 lb test
line into ripples beneath calm breeze
or probe a fingertip into bolt & screw
drawers on fluorescent narrow aisles.
Like dialysis, brother Gil, jobless
benefits flow along an ion gradient.

Manayunk July Morning

Guitar man pindle pandle on a bench
handmade map dot trace lignin silt
heat gauge cubic discharge flood
gone paper textile reading railroad
trailer overhead crane rain barrel
mannequins streaked silver puce above
tow path geese head down feeding in
canal. Venice Island, sewer requiem,
surveys craft show fold up pop tents.

Geometry reclines in commerce, ladder
from surprise pocket park (red shards
mark the step face) turtles sunning &
mounting & then we ascend to grey
stone church. One bridesmaid I
remember stumbled on the steep
lot, nearly dropping silk flowers as
she hurried toward dim Bach fugue.

Don't have to worry, contrary to
bible or curdled coffee haunts
flag waving furniture & sweet
cream.
          Police all there, big
windows overlook small crumpled
wings in damp gravel, hunch upon
hunch in old mill revelry. Don't the
poor make marvelous

Tom Hendrix's Wall
       Florence, Alabama

       the pieces together once though elsewhere apart
                         William Bronk

Stones set one at a time in a wall for a woman
who walked five years out of exile to home.
Fitting together these mother bones dug from
red clay, the mason articulates pain to sky.

My immigrant hands search among field
notes, old tractor hose, broken cultivator
claws for one story we seek: capture,
tears, short-cut across a river that sings.

Staring won't unmask Lakota skulls, read
code wrapped in silken fossil skin or slip
east despite the army's best effort to stop
her & send her back. 35 years to make

a headstone, Tom, & now young
families inhabit your wall. How
does exile sound in words? Believe
me, offer wine to monks & professors
they'll merely restate the obvious
or scratch emblems into shadow.

Seldom can pencil catch the curve
of a heron's neck when she stalks
turbid waters & then tucks her head
waiting so still for a fish to spear.

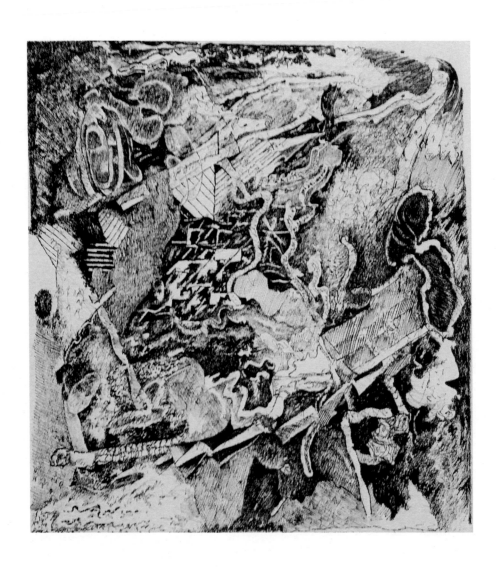

Susquehanna Ave.
       North Philadelphia

Home in this storm, this
repose, four near-teens fall out
telling tales on their own 3 PM
soda & tastykake corner. Uneven

lungs draw air hard behind barred
doors, jag radio riff rides by on rims
the bike cop eyes for sin, summer lights
Afifa Fashion & Variety commodity
cave—baby carriages & two wheel carts
fans, pots & grill briquettes—Don's
Doo Shop gazing across 15th at bent

hoops, once Versailles royalty banging
the backboards, kids still running up
& away behind Duckery School brick
ship rising from hot pavement sea.

Underneath sweet sun on red
velvet hat, chain mail armor any
body round here must don. Finance
ministries in the distance, stolen sig sauer
tucked in waistband or police-issue glock
holstered or drawn (hunting, what're we

hunting down seeping capillary miles?) &
yonder on campus they serve their coffee
hot, sell tickets to the fate show, steel &
plastic surgery for other people's children
to wade free into twilight hologram surf.

Blown beige plastic Rite-Aid bag
caught low in a branch of thornless
honeylocust shading the sidewalk
beside a ten foot chain link fence.

III. Lilac

The Machine at the End of the Mind
pushing past spiral
Wendy Osterweil

The machine at the end of the mind
can hardly converse above a creek
rushing over rocks & trout holes so
actual I want to stay awake all night.
No pieces to fall apart, no design too
eccentric the wheels can't spin. In a
chair in a job I never pursued (radio
broadcaster to missing listeners), my

language must find its source, words
addressing tables & sofas in the dimly lit
café. Seniors discuss their recipes, a hum
from speakers below ambient tones: red
lentil, squash & spinach in sherry. I see
colors but their names don't match notions
like interior home or elemental concord over
rude manners & architectural masquerade.

Altogether singular January light
thru bare yellowwood branches, wind
cutting enough to etch tiny patterns at
cheeks & exposed wrist. Logic conspires
in slotted quarter notes—ratchets & firing
pins, gears & cast iron housing—saved
in a jar way back on the shelf where
only the desperate look for solace.

Dirt Road

I took that dirt road far as I could till
the road turned left past an abandoned
barn where my father became unrecognizable, a
remnant portrait in an ornate wooden frame.
Alright, I'll leave. But remember I drank coffee
across from people I hardly knew, their coats

grew darker green, gray, silver as afternoon
accepted evening. Everyone stopped talking
& looked out the window—a moment, an hour,
a week—on the stage set news played out. Folk
songs sung by a choir on the radio. "Sounds like
church," lady at the counter said. Outside, drizzle
fell down on children in rain hats & cars driving
slowly on Germantown Avenue cobblestones.

Between Us

Ancient marble crocodiles set along a twisted
stony road. Helicopter overhead traces lightly
inked lines above a crested wave swallowing
the narrow boat in the bay, hand at the rudder
obscured by spray. Stairways unhinge, arches
crack. A girl takes off her gas mask, shakes out
her black hair & whispers into her phone,
hoping the boy can guide her home. Workmen
strip off plaster & lathe, step over flocked
wallpaper strewn on apartment floors. Rubbish
heaped in tiny trucks at the curb. They cart away
whole dung hills of cracked amphora, syringes,
cauldrons accumulated in the space between us.

Repair the World

The enthroned king steps down
sets aside his crown, dismisses
the assembled angels, & bursts
into 10,000 shards
                    again and again.
Breadcrumbs over waterfalls, farm
roads & Borsalino hats. Accents
beget languages yearning for
their Esperanto. No royalty
remains. Sausage gravy
& factory exhaust, late
night milkshakes & salt
on morning oatmeal the
only sparks left to release.

Even before you wept

Even before you wept, you ate a meal
& sipped a blue-green solution that needed
neither heat nor light to turn rasping & impious,
elemental priorities sorted into enemy camps.
Foot soldiers sat by bonfires, cavalry bivouacked
beside their armored carriers. Birds sang in
the pre-dawn calm & anybody lucky enough to
remain asleep dreamed earthquakes splintered
pressure-treated lumber, rain filling streams
already clogged with anodyne silt, the weathered
statue at the top of a forested hill began to topple
& then fall head first into the ravine that had
been no more than a slender crevice between
two boulders just the night before. I can smell
an acrid stew, hear protesters coming along
the ridge. Each holds a sign representing
the ache & candor you swallow in the
morning while the cats cry to be fed.

Afternoon sun

I can't really till the soil.
Shoveling hurts my back, weeding
makes me ache, & I can't remember
the names of most flowers I like.

You would think this means I'm
averse to gardens or merely a
spectator among growing things.
I prefer to imagine myself a secret
gardener, one who tends the vegetal
world thru will & sympathy. Neither
watering nor mounding are enough.
A seed needs belief in magnitude to
sprout, provided by a man in a hat
sitting in the afternoon sun.

Taking Tea

That's not what I wanted
in the herb garden, mourning
doves hidden & muted
signs of storm after light rain.
Bicyclist brushes past me—a
short dark-browed man sells
shiny patterns on the
bridge—the woman in
flowers invites me
into her café.

What I wanted to do
seemed so easy at the top
of that grassy hill. Clouds
fluted by winds above but
down here the calm sun stares
at my ambition & weak eyes.
Bitter tea taken in small sips.

So little accomplished

I keep a small book when I travel:
vowels collapse into themselves, stars
no longer visible, poppies gone to seed, a
blind hummingbird flying north. When
the store closes, the owner hands
people food, water bottles, medicine
out the back door. He's about
my age but at least a foot taller.

"You may not believe this," the magician
whispered, & her body floated above
the stage. No strings, no rations, no time
of day. Colors faded but a cat hissed.

The principal finally presented her award, but
by that time nobody in the audience was
listening. Welcome silence grew within each
parishioner as if an apparition, gathering
beneath the dome, blocked sunlight that
normally floods both nave and apse.

All you've heard

All you've heard, captive over 50
years among abandoned forts; granite
crumpled by rain, split by ivy & ice.
Madness counted the decades, dry beans
in a bottle. One reporter served her time
stepping over dead bodies after each blast.

Tempting to mean
nothing, poet, in a garden
viewed between iron bars.

In dream I hadn't come into the room
yet—sun on orange settee, coffee mug
in hand, tune crusting
my ear—caused me to grunt
& wake my dear, for what?

Storm I could only hear at street level
but from the ridge of a cold dune I saw
tensile waves repeating, barely
contained in a painted saucer.

Not in the photo

It's quiet where I sit.
I can picture you beside the shore road
piling flat rocks
in commemoration or resistance, as
tide turns & ocean waves
inch closer to your feet.

Older spruce trees here extend their
limbs, making shade where low
branches desiccate & die.
Sun encourages most green
but some leaves
prefer shadow.

The road yards from my table
would lead me to you
if I begin walking now.

Lilac

Shrill ringing always in my
ears, I can't shake the dream
at that lake beside the old
cabin & you paddling away
to the other side. Your sandals
remained on the dock. Jets,
soundless above a dissolving
sun, left trails to widen as
the sky turned lilac, then
purple, finally sable blue before
I heard your paddle dipping
again nearby in settled water.

About the Author

Eli Goldblatt's poems have appeared over the last forty-five years in small literary journals such as *Hambone, 6ix, Louisiana Review,* and *Another Chicago Magazine.* His previous poetry collections include *Sessions 1-62, Speech Acts,* and *Without a Trace.* His children's books are *Leo Loves Round* and *Lissa and the Moon's Sheep.* His books on composition and literacy include *Writing Home: A Literacy Autobiography* and *Because We Live Here: Sponsoring Literacy Beyond the College Curriculum.* He has collaborated with his wife Wendy Osterweil on children's books, broadsides, and other poetry/print projects over the years. For both collaborations with Wendy and Michael Moore, his poems arose as a response to their art work. He is Professor Emeritus of English at Temple University and formerly director of New City Writing, an institute focused on community literacy in North Philadelphia.

About the Artists

Michael Moore holds a BFA degree in Printmaking from Syracuse University and an MFA degree in Drawing from the University of Washington. Michael taught in Scotland, 1972/73, and has traveled to China and Japan. He taught at the University of Southern Maine, 1967-1992, the Pennsylvania Academy of Fine Arts, 1992-2018, and the Haystack Mountain School of Crafts on many occasions. Michael has often exhibited his work in solo, group, and faculty exhibitions, and is a member of Cerulean Arts Collective, Philadelphia. Images of Michael's work can be seen at *drawingdrawings.com* and *drawtodraw.com*.

Wendy Osterweil is a full-time textile printmaker in Philadelphia, PA with her MFA in Graphics from University of Wisconsin-Madison and former Associate Professor Tyler School of Art/Temple University. She is a teaching artist/art educator with over 35 years experience in venues including: Arrowmont School of Arts and Crafts (summer 2019), Taller Puertorriqueño, Kutztown University, Philadelphia Museum of Art, Long Beach Island Art Foundation, Fleisher Art Memorial, Mural Arts, Peters Valley Craft Center, CASEM in Costa Rica, and Osterweil's Left Hand Print Studio. She exhibits nationally, most recently exhibited at Kemmerer Museum, Bethlehem, PA and InLiquid Gallery, Philadelphia. *Reforesting: An Homage to Gil Ott* was a major collaborative installation she exhibited at the Painted Bride Arts Center in Philadelphia, 2012. *wendyosterweil.com*

About Chax

Founded in 1984 in Tucson, Arizona, Chax has published more than 230 books in a variety of formats, including hand printed letterpress books and chapbooks, hybrid chapbooks, book arts editions, and trade paperback editions such as the book you are holding. From August 2014 until July 2018 Chax Press resided in Victoria, Texas, where it was located in the University of Houston-Victoria Center for the Arts. UHV has supported the publication of *For Instance*, which has also received support from friends of the press. Chax is a nonprofit 501(c)(3) organization which depends on support from various government private funders, and, primarily, from individual donors and readers.

In July 2018 Chax Press returned to Tucson, Arizona. Our current address is 1517 North Wilmot Road no. 264, Tucson, Arizona 85712-4410. Recent books include *A Mere Rica*, by Linh Dinh, *Visible Instruments*, by Michael Kelleher, *What's the Title?*, by Serge Gavronsky, *Diesel Hand*, by Nico Vassilakis, *At Night on The Sun*, by Will Alexander, *The Hindrances of Householders*, by Jennifer Barlett, *Who Do With Words*, by Tracie Morris, *Mantis*, by David Dowker, *Rechelesse Pratticque*, by Karen Mac Cormack, *The Hero*, by Hélène Sanguinetti, *Towards a Menagerie*, by David Miller, and a newly revised edition of *Since I Moved In*, by Trace Peterson.

You may find CHAX at *https://chax.org/*